Lakshmi Chalisa

Lakshmi Chalisa

RUPA

Published in Sanskriti Press
Rupa Publications India Pvt. Ltd 2025
161-B/4, Gulmohar House,
Yusuf Sarai Community Centre,
New Delhi 110049

Sales centres:
Bengaluru Chennai
Hyderabad Kolkata Mumbai

P-ISBN: 978-93-7003-020-6
E-ISBN: 978-93-7003-203-3

First impression 2025

10 9 8 7 6 5 4 3 2 1

Printed in India

Contents

Introduction

The **Lakshmi Chalisa** is a revered forty-verse hymn (Chalisa) dedicated to **Goddess Lakshmi**, the Hindu goddess of wealth, prosperity, and divine grace. Reciting this Chalisa is a devotional practice embraced by millions of devotees, especially during auspicious occasions like **Diwali**, **Fridays**, **Purnima (full moon)**, and the **festivals of Lakshmi Puja and Varalakshmi Vratam**.

The word "**Chalisa**" comes from the Hindi word *"chalis"*, meaning **forty**, and refers to the number of verses in the hymn. Each verse glorifies the attributes, miracles, and the divine qualities of Goddess Lakshmi.

This poetic prayer seeks her blessings for material and spiritual abundance, protection from misfortunes, and inner peace.

Goddess Lakshmi, as described in the Chalisa, is more than just the giver of wealth. She embodies purity, righteousness, compassion, and divine wisdom. She is said to reside where virtue, cleanliness, and devotion flourish. Through the verses, devotees are reminded of her cosmic role—from being born during the churning of the ocean (*Samudra Manthan*), to serving Lord Vishnu in every incarnation, and to her powers that bestow **Riddhi (prosperity)**, **Siddhi (success)**, and **Bhakti (devotion)**.

Each verse of the **Lakshmi Chalisa** holds spiritual significance and is believed to remove obstacles, attract positive energy, and promote holistic well-being. Many devotees chant it daily or weekly, and often read it during **rituals, pujas, or fasting days**. It is a tool of devotion and meditation that draws the devotee closer to the divine feminine power.

Reading or listening to the Lakshmi Chalisa with **faith, focus, and humility** is believed to bring removal of financial difficulties and debts, blessings of wealth, harmony, and success, peace and stability in the household, fulfillment of righteous desires, and protection from negative forces and misfortunes.

In essence, the **Lakshmi Chalisa** is not just a prayer for riches, but a spiritual roadmap to contentment, grace, and higher consciousness—a way of inviting **Shri** (divine auspiciousness) into one's life.

Chalīsa

॥ दोहा ॥

मातु लक्ष्मी करि कृपा, करो हृदय में वास।
मनोकामना सिद्ध करि, परुवहु मेरी आस

Maatu Lakshmi kari kripa,
karo hriday mein vaas.
Manokamna siddh kari,
paruvahu meri aas.

Mother Lakshmi, with your grace, dwell in my heart.
Fulfill my desires, and grant me hope.

॥ सोरठा ॥

यही मोर अरदास, हाथ जोड़ विनती करुं।
सब विधि करौ सुवास, जय जननि जगदम्बिका।

Yahi mor ardaas, haath jod vinati karun.
Sab vidhi karau suvaas, Jai Janani Jagadambika.

This is my prayer, I fold my hands and humbly request.
Grant all good deeds, Hail the Mother of the Universe, Jagadambika.

॥ चौपाई ॥

सिन्धु सुता मैं सुमिरौ तोही।
ज्ञान, बुद्धि, विद्या दो मोही॥
तुम समान नहिं कोई उपकारी।
सब विधि पुरवहु आस हमारी॥

Sindhu suta main sumirau tohi.
Gyaan, buddhi, vidya do mohi.
Tum samaan nahin koi upkaari.
Sab vidhi purvahu aas hamari.

I remember you, O daughter of the ocean.
Grant me knowledge, wisdom, and
learning.
There is none as kind as you.
Fulfill all our hopes through your grace.

जय जय जगत जननि जगदम्बा।
सबकी तुम ही हो अवलम्बा।।
तुम ही हो सब घट घट वासी।
विनती यही हमारी खासी।।

Jai jai jagat janani Jagadamba.
Sabki tum hi ho avalamba.
Tum hi ho sab ghat ghat waasi.
Vinati yahi hamari khaasi.

Hail, Hail, the Mother of the Universe,
Jagadamba.
You are the support of all.
You reside in every heart and every being.
This is our humble plea.

जगजननी जय सिन्धु कुमारी।
दीनन की तुम हो हितकारी।।
विनवौं नित्य तुमहिं महारानी।
कृपा करौ जग जननि भवानी।।

Jagjanani Jai Sindhu Kumari.
Deenan ki tum ho hitkaari.
Vinavon nitya tumhin mahaarani.
Kripa karau jag janani bhavani.

Hail the Mother of the Universe, O
Daughter of the Ocean.
You are the benefactor of the poor and
the needy.
I pray to you daily, O Queen of the
Universe.
Bestow your grace, O Mother of the
World, Bhavani.

केहि विधि स्तुति करौं तिहारी।
सुधि लीजै अपराध बिसारी।।
कृपा दृष्टि चितववो मम ओरी।
जगजननी विनती सुन मोरी।।

Kehi vidhi stuti karon tihari.
Sudhi leejay apradh bisari.
Kripa drishti chitavo mam ori.
Jagjanani vinati sun mori.

How should I praise you, O Mother?
Forgive my sins and grant me your wisdom.
Look upon me with your grace, O Mother.
Listen to my plea, O Mother of the Universe.

ज्ञान बुद्धि जय सुख की दाता।
संकट हरो हमारी माता।।
क्षीरसिन्धु जब विष्णु मथायो।
चौदह रत्न सिन्धु में पायो।।

Gyaan buddhi jai sukh ki daata.
Sankat haro hamari mata.
Ksheersindhu jab Vishnu mathayo.
Chaudah ratna sindhu mein paayo.

You are the giver of wisdom, intelligence,
and happiness.
Remove our troubles, O Mother.
When Vishnu churned the ocean,
He obtained fourteen gems from it.

चौदह रत्न में तुम सुखरासी।
सेवा कियो प्रभु बनि दासी।।
जब जब जन्म जहां प्रभु लीन्हा।
रुप बदल तहं सेवा कीन्हा।।

Chaudah ratna mein tum sukhraasi.
Seva kiyo prabhu ban daasi.
Jab jab janm jahan prabhu leenha.
Roop badal tahin seva keenha.

Among the fourteen gems, you are the
treasure of happiness.
You served the Lord as his devotee.
Whenever the Lord took birth,
You changed your form and served him.

स्वयं विष्णु जब नर तनु धारा।
लीन्हेउ अवधपुरी अवतारा।।
तब तुम प्रगट जनकपुर माहीं।
सेवा कियो हृदय पुलकाहीं।।

Swayam Vishnu jab nar tanu dhaara.
Leenhe Avadhpuri avatar.
Tab tum prakat Janakpur maahin.
Seva kiyo hriday pulkaahin.

When Vishnu himself incarnated in
human form,
He took the avatar in Ayodhya.
Then you appeared in Janakpur,
And served with a heart full of joy.

अपनाया तोहि अन्तर्यामी।
विश्व विदित त्रिभुवन की स्वामी।।
तुम सम प्रबल शक्ति नहीं आनी।
कहं लौ महिमा कहौं बखानी।।

Apnaya tohi antaryami.
Vishw vidit tribhuvan ki swami.
Tum sam prabal shakti nahin aani.
Kahun lau mahima kahon bakhaani.

You made me your own, O Lord of the
Universe,
You are the master of all three worlds,
known to all.
There is no power as great as yours.
How can I describe your greatness?

मन क्रम वचन करै सेवकाई।
मन इच्छित वांछित फल पाई।।
तजि छल कपट और चतुराई।
पूजहिं विविध भाँति मनलाई।।

Man kram vachan karai sevakai.
Man ichhit vanchhit phal paai.
Taji chhal kapat aur chaturai.
Pujahim vivid bhaanti manlaai.

One who serves you with heart, mind, and words,
Will receive the desired results, fulfilling all wishes.
Renouncing deceit, cunning, and trickery,
One worships you in various ways with a sincere mind.

और हाल मैं कहौं बुझाई।
जो यह पाठ करै मन लाई।।
ताको कोई कष्ट नोई।
मन इच्छित पावै फल सोई।।

Aur haal main kahun bujhaai.
Jo yah paath karai man laai.
Tako koi kasht noyi.
Man ichhit paavai phal soi.

If someone reads this with devotion,
They will be blessed with understanding.
Such a person will not face any hardships,
They will attain the fruits of their desires.

त्राहि त्राहि जय दुःख निवारिणि।
त्रिविध ताप भव बन्धन हारिणी।।
जो चालीसा पढ़ै पढ़ावै।
ध्यान लगाकर सुनै सुनावै।।

Trahi trahi jai dukh nivarini.
Trividha taap bhav bandhan haarini.
Jo chalisa padhae padhavae.
Dhyaan lagakar sunai sunavae

Hail, Hail, O remover of sorrow,
You destroy the three types of pain and the bonds of life.
Whoever reads, recites, listens, and meditates on this Chalisa,
They will be blessed with peace and prosperity.

ताकौ कोई न रोग सतावै।
पुत्र आदि धन सम्पत्ति पावै।।
पुत्रहीन अरु सम्पति हीना।
अन्ध बधिर कोढ़ी अति दीना।।

Tako koi na rog sataavai.
Putra aadi dhan sampatti paavai.
Putraheen aru sampatti heena.
Andha badhir kodhi ati deena.

No disease will trouble such a person,
They will attain wealth, children, and prosperity.
Those without children or wealth,
The blind, the deaf, and the diseased will be cured.

विप्र बोलाय कै पाठ करावै।
शंका दिल में कभी न लावै।।
पाठ करावै दिन चालीसा।
ता पर कृपा करैं गौरीसा।।

Vipra bolaye kay paath karavae.
Shanka dil mein kabhi na laavae.
Paath karavai din chalisa.
Ta par kripa karain Gaurisa.

The Brahmin recites and makes others recite,
Never let doubts enter your heart.
One who recites the Chalisa daily,
Will receive the blessings of Goddess Gauri.

सुख सम्पत्ति बहुत सी पावै।
कमी नहीं काहू की आवै।।
बारह मास करै जो पूजा।
तेहि सम धन्य और नहिं दूजा।।

Sukh sampatti bahut si paavai.
Kami nahin kaahu ki aavai.
Baarah maas karai jo pooja.
Tehi sam dhanya aur nahin dooja.

Such a person will gain immense wealth
and happiness,
They will not lack anything in life.
One who worships daily for twelve
months,
Is as blessed as none other.

प्रतिदिन पाठ करै मन माही।
उन सम कोइ जग में कहुं नाहीं।।
बहुविधि क्या मैं करौं बड़ाई।
लेय परीक्षा ध्यान लगाई।।

Pratidin paath karai mann maahi.
Un sam koi jag mein kahu nahin.
Bahuvidhi kya main karun badaai.
Ley pariksha dhyaan lagaai.

Those who recite this daily with devotion,
There is no one like them in the world.
What can I praise in many ways?
Only by focusing and meditating can the greatness be understood.

करि विश्वास करै व्रत नेमा।
होय सिद्ध उपजै उर प्रेमा।।
जय जय जय लक्ष्मी भवानी।
सब में व्यापित हो गुण खानी।।

Kari vishwas karai vrat nema.
Hoy siddh upajai ur prema.
Jai jai jai Lakshmi Bhavani.
Sab mein vyaapit ho gun khani.

By having faith and following vows and rules,
One achieves success and love arises in their heart.
Hail, hail, hail Goddess Lakshmi,
You are present in everything, and your virtues are abundant.

तुम्हरो तेज प्रबल जग माहीं।
तुम सम कोउ दयालु कहुं नाहिं।।
मोहि अनाथ की सुधि अब लीजै।
संकट काटि भक्ति मोहि दीजै।।

Tumharo teja prabal jag maahi.
Tum sam kou dayaalu kahu naahin.
Mohi anath ki sudhi ab leejai.
Sankat kaati bhakti mohi deejai.

Your radiance is supreme in the world,
There is no one as compassionate as you.
Please take care of me, the helpless one,
Remove my troubles and grant me devotion.

भूल चूक करि क्षमा हमारी।
दर्शन दजै दशा निहारी।।
बिन दर्शन व्याकुल अधिकारी।
तुमहि अछत दु:ख सहते भारी।।

Bhool chook kari kshama hamari.
Darshan dajai dasha nihari.
Bin darshan vyakul adhikaari.
Tumhi achhat dukh sahte bhaari.

Please forgive our mistakes,
Look upon us with grace and consider our condition.
Without your sight, the deserving ones suffer in anguish,
But with your grace, all pain is alleviated.

नहिं मोहिं ज्ञान बुद्धि है तन में।
सब जानत हो अपने मन में।।
रुप चतुर्भुज करके धारण।
कष्ट मोर अब करहु निवारण।।

Nahin mohin gyaan buddhi hai tan mein.
Sab jaanat ho apne man mein.
Roop chaturbhuj karke dhaaran.
Kasht mor ab karahu nivaran.

I do not possess knowledge and wisdom
within myself,
But you know everything within your
mind.
You take the form of the four-armed one,
Now remove my suffering and troubles.

केहि प्रकार मैं करौं बड़ाई।
ज्ञान बुद्धि मोहि नहिं अधिकाई।।

Kehi prakar main karun badaai.
Gyaan buddhi mohi nahin adhikaai.

In what way can I praise you?
I do not have the knowledge and wisdom
to do so.

॥ दोहा ॥

त्राहि त्राहि दुःख हारिणी, हरो वेगि सब त्रास।
जयति जयति जय लक्ष्मी, करो शत्रु को नाश॥

Doha

Trahi trahi dukh haarini,
Haro vegi sab traas.
Jayati jayati jay Lakshmi,
Karo shatrū ko naash.

Hail, Hail, O remover of sorrow, Quickly remove all distress.
Victory, victory, victory to Goddess Lakshmi, Destroy all enemies.

रामदास धरि ध्यान नित, विनय करत कर जोर।
मातु लक्ष्मी दास पर, करहु दया की कोर।।

Ramdas dhari dhyaan nit,
Vinay karat kar zor.
Matṛ Lakshmi das par,
Karahu daya ki kor.

Holding Ramdas in my thoughts,
I humbly pray with devotion.
O Mother Lakshmi, show mercy to your servant,
Bless him with your kindness.

आरती श्री लक्ष्मी जी

ॐ जय लक्ष्मी माता, मैया जय लक्ष्मी माता ।
तुमको निशिदिन सेवत, हरि विष्णु विधाता ।।
ॐ जय लक्ष्मी माता ।।

उमा, रमा, ब्रह्माणी, तुम ही जग-माता ।
सूर्य-चन्द्रमा ध्यावत, नारद ऋषि गाता ।।
ॐ जय लक्ष्मी माता ।।

दुर्गा रुप निरंजनी, सुख सम्पत्ति दाता ।
जो कोई तुमको ध्यावत, ऋद्धि-सिद्धि धन पाता ।।
ॐ जय लक्ष्मी माता ।।

तुम पाताल-निवासिनि, तुम ही शुभदाता ।
कर्म-प्रभाव-प्रकाशिनी, भवनिधि की त्राता ॥
ॐ जय लक्ष्मी माता ॥

जिस घर में तुम रहतीं, सब सद्‌गुण आता ।
सब सम्भव हो जाता, मन नहीं घबराता ॥
ॐ जय लक्ष्मी माता ॥

तुम बिन यज्ञ न होते, वस्त्र न कोई पाता ।
खान-पान का वैभव, सब तुमसे आता ॥
ॐ जय लक्ष्मी माता ॥

शुभ-गुण मन्दिर सुन्दर, क्षीरोदधि-जाता ।
रत्न चतुर्दश तुम बिन, कोई नहीं पाता ॥
ॐ जय लक्ष्मी माता ॥

महालक्ष्मीजी की आरती, जो कोई जन गाता ।

उर आनन्द समाता, पाप उतर जाता ।।

ॐ जय लक्ष्मी माता ।।

Aarti Shri Lakshmiji ki

Om Jai Lakshmi Mata,
Maiya Jai Lakshmi Mata ।
Tumko nishidin sevat,
Hari Vishnu Vidhata ।।

Om Jai Lakshmi Mata ।।

Uma, Rama, Brahmani,
Tum hi Jag-Mata ।
Surya-Chandrama dhyavat,
Narad Rishi gata ।।

Om Jai Lakshmi Mata ।।

Durga roop Niranjani,
Sukh sampatti data ।
Jo koi tumko dhyavat,
Riddhi-Siddhi dhan pata ॥

Om Jai Lakshmi Mata ॥

Tum Patal-nivasini,
Tum hi Shubhdāta ।
Karm-prabhav-prakashini,
Bhavanidhi ki trata ॥

Om Jai Lakshmi Mata ॥

Jis ghar mein tum rahti,
Sab sadgun ata ।
Sab sambhav ho jata,
Man nahin ghabrata ॥

Om Jai Lakshmi Mata ॥

Tum bin yajna na hote,
Vastr na koi pata ।
Khan-paan ka vaibhav,
Sab tumse ata ॥

Om Jai Lakshmi Mata ॥

Shubh-gun mandir sundar,
Kshirodadhi-jata ।
Ratna chaturdash tum bin,
Koi nahin pata ॥

Om Jai Lakshmi Mata ॥

Mahalakshmiji ki aarti,
Jo koi jan gata ।
Ur anand samata,
Paap utar jata ॥

Om Jai Lakshmi Mata ॥

Aarti Shri Lakshmi Ji

Om, Victory to Mother Lakshmi,
O Mother, Victory to You!

Day and night, You are served
By Lord Vishnu, the Creator

Om, Victory to Mother Lakshmi

Uma, Rama, Brahmani—
You are the Mother of the Universe

The Sun and Moon meditate on You,
And Sage Narada sings Your praises

Om, Victory to Mother Lakshmi

In the form of Durga, the pure one,
You are the giver of happiness and wealth

Whoever meditates on You,
Receives prosperity, success, and riches

Om, Victory to Mother Lakshmi

You dwell in the netherworld,
And bring auspicious blessings

Revealer of karmic effects,
You are the savior from worldly suffering

Om, Victory to Mother Lakshmi

In the home where You reside,
All virtues arrive

Everything becomes possible,
And the mind never fears

Om, Victory to Mother Lakshmi

Without You, no sacrifices occur,
No one obtains clothes

All food and luxury
Come from You alone

Om, Victory to Mother Lakshmi

Beautiful temple of auspicious qualities,
Born from the ocean of milk

Without You, none can obtain
The fourteen precious gems

Om, Victory to Mother Lakshmi

Whoever sings this Aarti
Of Mahalakshmi with devotion

Their heart fills with joy,
And sins are washed away

Om, Victory to Mother Lakshmi